SCHOLASTIC BOOK GUIDES
Tuck Everlasting
BY NATALIE BABBITT

Scholastic grants teachers permission to photocopy the reproducible pages from this book for classroom use. No other part of this publication may be reproduced in whole or in part, or stored in a retrieval system, or transmitted in any form or by any means, electronic, mechanical, photocopying, recording, or otherwise, without permission of the publisher. For information regarding permission, write to Scholastic Teaching Resources, 524 Broadway, New York, NY 10012-3999.

Written by Linda Ward Beech
Cover design by Maria Lilja
Interior design by Drew Hires
Interior illustrations by Jenny Williams
Photograph of Natalie Babbitt by Avi

ISBN 0-439-57285-1
Copyright © 2003, 1997 by Scholastic Inc.
All rights reserved.
Printed in the U.S.A.

1 2 3 4 5 6 7 8 9 10 31   09 08 07 06 05 04 03

NEW YORK • TORONTO • LONDON • AUCKLAND • SYDNEY
MEXICO CITY • NEW DELHI • HONG KONG • BUENOS AIRES

SCHOLASTIC Teaching *Resources*

Table of Contents

BEFORE READING THE BOOK
Summary 3
Characters 3
About the Author 4
Vocabulary 4
Notes About Fantasy 5
Getting Started 5

EXPLORING THE BOOK
Chapters 1 – 9
Summary and Discussion Questions 6
Cross-Curricular Activities: Language Arts,
Art, Science 7
Chapters 10 – 19
Summary and Discussion Questions 8
Cross-Curricular Activities: Writing,
Science, Science 9
Chapters 20 – Epilogue
Summary and Discussion Questions 10
Cross-Curricular Activities: Social Studies,
Writing 11

SUMMARIZING THE BOOK
Putting It All Together 12
Class, Group, Partner, and Individual Projects 12
Evaluation Ideas 13

STUDENT REPRODUCIBLES
Working With Words 14
And Then 15
Where Do You Stand? 16

Answers for Worksheets 13

Before Reading the Book

SUMMARY

On a lazy summer day, 10-year-old Winnie Foster battles boredom by taking a walk in the wood that her family owns near Treegap. There, she sees Jesse Tuck drinking from a spring. When Winnie tries to drink from it too, Jesse stops her. Soon after he, his brother Miles, and mother Mae kidnap Winnie and take her to their home. Winnie soon learns the story of the Tucks who have all drunk from the spring and are now ageless; they will never die. The Tucks try to make Winnie understand how terrible it would be if others found out about their secret. Angus Tuck, especially, seems saddened and burdened by the family's plight. Meanwhile, unknown to Winnie and the Tucks, a stranger in a yellow suit has followed them, stolen their horse, and reported Winnie's whereabouts to her family.  The stranger blackmails Winnie's parents; in return for the wood, he will save Winnie, and bring her home. When the man returns to the Tucks bragging about his plans for the spring water, Mae kills him. The constable puts her in jail, but Winnie and the other Tucks manage to rescue her. They know that if Mae is hung from the gallows, she won't die. Jesse gives Winnie a bottle of water from the spring and asks her to drink it when she is 17 so that they can be married and live together forever. Although she loves Jesse, Winnie pours the water on a toad that she has befriended. Years later, Mae and Angus Tuck return to Treegap and find Winnie's grave in the cemetery.

STORY CHARACTERS

People

Winifred (Winnie) Foster	10-year-old girl who loves the Tuck family
Mae Tuck	Wife of Angus Tuck
Angus Tuck	Known as Tuck; Mae's husband
Miles Tuck	Older son of Mae and Tuck
Jesse Tuck	Younger son of Mae and Tuck
Granny	Winnie's grandmother
Mr. and Mrs. Foster	Winnie's parents
Stranger	Man in the yellow suit
Constable	Keeper of the law in Treegap
Anna	Daughter of Miles Tuck

ABOUT THE AUTHOR

Natalie Babbitt grew up wanting to be a writer and an illustrator and has fulfilled this childhood dream. The first book she illustrated was written by her husband and called *The Forty-Ninth Magician.* Her first novel was *The Search for Delicious,* which she describes as a "complicated fairy tale." Many of Babbitt's other books are also fantasies set in the past. She works hard at using accurate descriptions in her books. For example, when writing *Eyes of the Amaryllis,* a book set in nineteenth-century Cape Cod, Babbitt did a lot of research on hurricanes which play an important role in the story. She also consulted tide charts of the period. To Babbitt, writing is "hard, hard work." She advocates ceaseless reading for those who aspire to such a career.

LITERATURE CONNECTIONS
Other books by Natalie Babbitt include:
- *The Search for Delicious*
- *Kneeknock Rose*
- *Goody Hall*
- *The Devil's Storybook*
- *The Eyes of the Amaryllis*

VOCABULARY
Like the work of other exceptional authors, Natalie Babbitt's book will stretch students' vocabulary. Following are words from the story with which students may need help. Challenge students to alphabetize the words and compile them into a glossary to use while reading *Tuck Everlasting.* You may also wish to hand out the reproducible on page 14 at this time.

balmy	submission	patent
tangent	indomitable	petulance
tranquil	eddies	unflinchingly
bovine	perilous	acrid
contemplation	cavernous	exertion
melancholy	mirage	gingerly
rueful	trill	ponderous
bristly	elation	remorseless
intrusions	skittering	plaintive
grimace	anguish	prostrate
exasperated	barbarian	curliecues
jaunty	illiterate	ebbed
self-deprecation	constable	furrowed
remnants	roust	protruding
galling	cahoots	perversely

amber	accommodations	constricted
pruned	gallows	accomplice
burly	circuit judge	staunchly
fidgeted	teeming	revulsion
implored	searing	lounged
reservoirs	surveyed	catholic
colander	metaphysics	verandah

NOTES ABOUT FANTASY

Discuss with the class the difference between a fantasy and a realistic novel. Mention other examples of fantasies including fairy tales with which students are familiar. Point out that magic is an important component of many fantasies. Encourage students to list possible characteristics of a fantasy in their writing journals and to consult these as they read *Tuck Everlasting*.

GETTING STARTED

You might use one or more of these ideas as you introduce the book to the class:

• Discuss the different reasons that people have secrets. Talk about how certain information can sometimes be harmful to people. Tell students that a secret is at the centerpiece of the book.

• Ask students what they think of when they hear the word "everlasting." Note their responses, then point out that this word is used in the title of the book they are about to read. Write the title on the chalkboard.

• Draw a circle on the board and add spokes to make it a wheel. Ask students to brainstorm things that are circles as you write them on the board. Explain that circles are a symbol in *Tuck Everlasting* and tell students to consider how they are used as they read.

• Lastly, read aloud the prologue at the beginning of the book. What mood does the author set with the prologue? Tell students to keep in mind the three "unrelated" things that the author mentions as they read the book.

TEACHER TIP

Ask students to decide, as they read the book, whether the secret in this story is one that should be kept.

Exploring the Book

CHAPTERS 1–9

WHAT HAPPENS

Mae Tuck sets out to meet her sons, Jesse and Miles, for their 10-year reunion near Treegap. Meanwhile, Winnie Foster, bored and cross, tells a toad that she will soon run away. That evening, a stranger in a yellow suit comes by the foster home and stops to ask some questions. As they talk, they hear music coming from the nearby wood. The next day Winnie goes walking in the wood which is owned by her family. She comes across Jesse Tuck sitting under a large tree and drinking from a spring. When Winnie tries to drink, Jesse stops her. Then Mae and Miles appear. Alarmed at Winnie's discovery of the spring, they kidnap her. Winnie learns that the music she heard comes from Mae's music box. She also learns the Tucks' secret: the water in the spring is magic and has made them ageless. They are all exactly the same age as the day they first drank it many years ago. Despite her worry at being kidnapped, Winnie finds the Tucks kind and rather sweet. At their home, she meets Angus, the father.

QUESTIONS TO TALK ABOUT

COMPREHENSION AND RECALL

1. Why is Winnie discontent at the beginning of the story? (*She's an only child who is watched all the time and has to obey lots of rules. She would like to get out and explore.*)

2. Why is Winnie afraid to run away? (*She's been told it would be dangerous; she believes it would be.*)

3. Why does Winnie talk to the toad? (*She's lonely; has no one else to talk to.*)

4. Why doesn't Jesse want Winnie to drink from the spring? (*He says it will be bad for her; there's something he doesn't want her to know.*)

HIGHER LEVEL THINKING SKILLS

5. What does Mae mean when she says, "The worst is happening at last."? (*Their secret is out.*)

6. How could someone look exactly the same for 87 years? (*Possible: magic*)

7. Why does the stranger remind Winnie of funeral ribbons? (*Possible: something about him seems sinister or unpleasant.*)

8. Why doesn't Winnie ask the man in the yellow suit for help when she is being kidnapped? (*Possible: She doesn't trust him; isn't really afraid of the Tucks; is having an adventure at last; isn't thinking clearly.*)

9. Why does Winnie feel reassured when she hears the music box? (*She's heard the music before; it connects her to home. The box is pretty and she doesn't think someone who owned it could be too terrible.*)

10. Why does Winnie begin to feel happy about being kidnapped? (*She starts to think of the Tucks as her special friends; is no longer afraid and alone; thinks living forever is exciting.*)

11. Why do you think the stranger is following Winnie and the Tucks? (*Possible: He plans to harm Winnie or the Tucks; he is interested in the spring.*)

LITERARY ELEMENTS
12. Characterization: How does the author show that the Fosters aren't very neighborly? (*They live in a cottage with a "touch-me-not-appearance." They don't let Winnie out to play, and aren't friendly to strangers. People aren't supposed to go in their wood.*)

13. Genre: What part of the story is fantasy? (*The Tucks will live forever because of the spring water.*)

PERSONAL RESPONSE
14. Winnie learns an incredible story from the Tucks. How would you have felt about it? What would you have done?

15. Mae has a music box as her special possession. What special possession do you have?

CROSS-CURRICULAR ACTIVITIES
LANGUAGE ARTS: *Listen to the Language*
Draw students' attention to the superb imagery that the author creates in this story. You might use as examples her description of the peak of summer in the prologue, the picture of a sunset she paints in Chapter 4, or the setting for the Tucks' home in Chapter 9. Review with students literary devices such as simile, metaphor, and personification. Ask students to identify the following from the story, then have them find additional examples of each.
- "her backbone felt like a pipe full of cold running water" (simile)
- "the sun is the hub of the wheeling calendar" (metaphor)
- "the sun was only just opening its own eye on the eastern horizon" (personification)
- "Mae sat there frowning, a great potato of a woman" (metaphor)
- "he had a kind of grace, like a well-handled marionette" (simile)

ART: *See the Similes*
Suggest that students illustrate some of the literary devices they locate in the story. They might make a chart as shown here, including a literal and a figurative illustration for each literary device.

Literary Device	Literary Illustration	Figurative Illustration
"the music . . . was like a ribbon tying her to familiar things"		
"the toad . . . plopped its heavy mudball of a body"		

SCIENCE: *Looking at Life Cycles*
Point out that death is part of the life cycle of living things; nothing lives forever. Have students work in groups to investigate various kinds of life cycles. For example, they might look at the life cycle of a plant that grows from seed; a plant that grows from a tuber; an insect such as a butterfly; a bird; a mammal. Have students compare the different life cycles and note the role that death plays in each.

CHAPTERS 10 – 19

WHAT HAPPENS

Although uneasy at first, Winnie finds warmth and comfort with the Tucks. She is particularly drawn to the kindly father who's called Tuck. Out on the pond, in his rowboat, Tuck explains how his family has "dropped off the wheel" and are stuck because they will never die. That night, Jesse suggests that Winnie drink some spring water when she is 17 so they can get married and live together forever. The next morning, out on the pond with Miles, Winnie has trouble thinking about death, even that of a fish Miles has caught. Meanwhile, the man in the yellow suit has followed the Tucks home, stolen their horse, and, in exchange for Winnie's return, blackmailed the Fosters into selling him their wood. The man arrives again at the Tucks' home and announces that he owns the wood and will sell the spring water. He wants the Tucks to help him demonstrate its power. When the Tucks refuse, he grabs Winnie and says he will use her instead, after she drinks form the spring. Mae hits him with a shotgun on the back of his skull, just as the constable arrives.

QUESTIONS TO TALK ABOUT
COMPREHENSION AND RECALL

1. How do the Tucks show kindness to Winnie? (*They come to see her at night and tell her how much they like having her with them.*)

2. How does the man in the yellow suit blackmail the Fosters? (*He says he'll bring back Winnie if they sell him the wood.*)

3. Why is the constable surprised that the Fosters agree to sell the wood? (*He says they're proud—"family-proud and land-proud."*)

4. What is the motive of the man in the yellow suit? (*He wants to use the spring to make a fortune and have power.*)

HIGHER LEVEL THINKING SKILLS

5. Why has living forever not always been fun for the Tucks? (*Miles lost his wife and children; people think they are strange and shun them; they can never stay in one place.*)

6. Why does Winnie say she wants to go home? (*She's suddenly homesick; has never been away before. She sees how different life at the Tucks' house is from her own home.*)

7. How is the pond water like life itself? (*It's always moving on, changing.*)

8. Why does Tuck say he and his family are "like rocks beside the road?" (*They're not living, growing, or changing; they are just there.*)

9. Why is it so important for Winnie to understand and keep the Tucks' secret? (*If others find the spring and drink from it, their lives will be frozen in time also.*)

10. Why doesn't Winnie want to fish? (*She's upset at the thought of death.*)

11. Why does Winnie think that Tuck is the "dearest of them all?" (*Possible: He is kind and so truly wretched at their fate and the dangers to others.*)

LITERARY ELEMENTS

12. Foreshadowing: Why does the author say, "Across the pond a bullfrog spoke a deep note of warning" when Winnie and Tuck go out in the rowboat? (*The bullfrog foreshadows trouble ahead.*)

13. Significant detail: Why does the author put the stranger in a yellow suit? (*Possible: It makes the reader notice him and understand that he is different.*)

PERSONAL RESPONSE

14. What is your reaction to the Tucks' home? Is it a place you would like to be?

15. Have you ever been homesick? How did you feel?

16. What do you think about Jesse's offer to Winnie? Would you agree to drink the water? Should Winnie?

17. How do you feel about Mae's reaction to the stranger?

CROSS-CURRICULAR ACTIVITIES

WRITING: *Different Points of View*

Discuss with the class the ways in which Miles and Jesse differ in their personalities, outlooks, and appearances. Then have students write compare and contrast paragraphs about the two young men.

As an alternate assignment, students might compare the outlooks of Tuck and Mae regarding their fate. Have students begin by rereading and discussing these quotes:
  Mae: "Life's got to be lived, no matter how long or short."
  Tuck: "Living's heavy work, but off to one side, the way *we* are, it's useless, too."

SCIENCE: *Using Your Senses*

Remind students how important the five senses are when it comes to communication. Have students think of ways that they use their senses for everyday tasks. Then point out that good writers often tap a reader's senses to make a book more vivid. Have students make charts such as the one shown here, and then fill them in using different examples from the book.

SIGHT	"The sky was a ragged blaze of red and pink and orange"
SOUND	"The hard heels of her buttoned boots made a hollow banging sound"
TOUCH	"It was rough and soft, both at once. And cool."
TASTE	"I'm about dry as dust."
SMELL	"The air was cooler and smelled agreeably damp"

SCIENCE: *The Water Cycle*

In Chapter 12, Tuck describes the water cycle in his effort to explain life and death to Winnie. Students might make labeled diagrams showing the water cycle.

TEACHER TIP

Ask students why they think the man in the yellow suit has no name. What name would they give him?

CHAPTERS 20 – EPILOGUE

WHAT HAPPENS

The constable takes Mae to the local jail. Winnie tells him that she wasn't kidnapped but chose to go with the Tucks. Back home, Winnie realizes that Mae meant to kill the stranger because of the spring. She also realizes that Mae can't go to the gallows because she won't die. When Jesse tells her about their plan to rescue Mae, Winnie offers to help by taking Mae's place in the jail so the constable won't know about the escape right away. During a fierce storm, Winnie and the Tucks rescue Mae. The Tucks disappear from Treegap. Winnie finds she has earned an interesting reputation among other children in town. One day the toad reappears and is threatened by a dog. Winnie rescues the toad, then pours the spring water Jesse has given her on it. She has made the decision not to live forever and marry Jesse. Almost 70 years later, Mae and Tuck return to Treegap and find Winnie's grave.

QUESTIONS TO TALK ABOUT

COMPREHENSION AND RECALL

1. Why does Winnie tell the constable that she wasn't kidnapped? (*She now thinks of the Tucks as her friends and doesn't want them to get in trouble.*)

2. How does Winnie help Mae escape? (*She takes Mae's place in the jail so the constable won't know Mae has gone right away.*)

3. How does Winnie's image in the village change after she helps Mae? (*Children come by to see her and are impressed. They used to think she was too prissy.*)

HIGHER LEVEL THINKING SKILLS

4. Why does Tuck stare "entranced" at the man in the yellow suit after Mae hits him? (*He's jealous. The man is near death.*)

5. Why is Tuck distressed about Mae being hung on the gallows? (*When she doesn't die, everyone will know the secret.*)

6. How do you think the Fosters feel about the stranger's death? (*Probably relieved—they won't have to sell their wood.*)

7. Why is Winnie conflicted about helping Mae escape? (*She knows it's important, but she doesn't want to deceive her family again.*)

8. Why does Winnie save the toad from the dog? (*She thinks of it as hers because she's seen it often before. She doesn't want it to die.*)

9. Why does Tuck say, "Good girl" when he sees that Winnie is dead? (*He knows she didn't drink the spring water. He believes she made the right choice.*)

10. What important decision does Winnie make when she pours the spring water on the toad? (*She won't drink it herself, nor live forever, nor marry Jesse.*)

LITERARY ELEMENTS
11. Foreshadowing: How does the author foreshadow the use of Tuck's gun? (*It's mentioned in the description of their home.*)

12. Symbolism: How does the author connect Winnie and the Tucks at the end of the story? (*The Tucks find Winnie's grave and see the toad that, like them, will never die.*)

PERSONAL RESPONSE
13. Is Jesse being selfish when he gives Winnie the bottle of spring water?

14. How does the ending make you feel?

CROSS-CURRICULAR ACTIVITIES
SOCIAL STUDIES: *The Years Make a Difference*
Point out to students that almost 70 years pass before the Tucks return to Treegap. Discuss some of the changes that they find. Then have students find out about changes in your community in the last 70 years. Suggest that students interview older citizens who have witnessed these changes or visit a local historical society or library to read about them. Students might use their findings in a bulletin board display.

WRITING: *A Fantasy*
Invite students to explore the idea of living forever in a story of their own. Have students read their stories aloud to the class, then lead a discussion on their topic and point of view.

Summarizing the Book

PUTTING IT ALL TOGETHER
Use one or more of the following activities to help students summarize and review *Tuck Everlasting*.

CLASS PROJECT: *The Picture Book Version*
Students might work together to create a picture book version of *Tuck Everlasting* that they can share with a younger grade. You might assign each student a chapter to illustrate or have students work in groups to cover several chapters. You might also ask half of the class to be writers and the other half to illustrate the new story. Enlist students' ideas in deciding on an approach to complete the project.

GROUP PROJECT: *Say It with Music*
Discuss how the author uses words to create different moods in the book. Point out that music also creates moods. Then have students work in groups to select music to represent different events and moods in the story. The groups can take turns playing their music for the class. Have each group introduce the music by summarizing the part of the story it relates to.

PARTNER PROJECT: *What Does It Mean?*
Assign students to work with partners. Each partner should find five interesting sentences from the book and write them on five separate pieces of paper. Then, have the partners exchange papers and write—in their own words—what they think the sentences mean. If a student chooses a sentence that is a quotation, they might ask their partner to identify the speaker. Encourage students to follow up by discussing the sentences and interpretations.

TEACHER TIP
Check your local video store's reference catalog to find a listing for *Tuck Everlasting*. Plan to show the video after students finish the book and then have them compare the two versions.

INDIVIDUAL PROJECT: *The Road to Treegap*
Some students might enjoy making illustrated maps of Treegap and its surroundings. Suggest that they reread Chapter 1 before beginning their project. Students can use the finished maps to retell the events of the book.

EVALUATION IDEAS
Ask students to come up with sets of rubrics to use in assessing one of the summarizing projects. For example, a rubric for a map of Treegap might include these objectives:
- Did the student demonstrate a close reading of the text?
- Did the student show originality in interpreting the setting?
- Did the student include enough details?
- Did the student execute the assignment with care?

Possible Answers for Worksheets
page 14: 1. c; synonyms 2. d; synonyms 3. b; synonyms 4. a; antonyms 5. b; antonyms 6. d; antonyms 7. a; antonyms 8. c; synonyms
page 15: 1. Cause/The Tucks drink from the spring. 2. Effect/The Tucks kidnap Winnie. 3. Cause/The Fosters want Winnie back. 4. Effect/Mae kills him. 5. Effect/Winnie and the Tucks rescue her. 6. Effect/Local children come to see her. 7. Cause/Winnie pours the spring water on the toad.
page 16: Students' bar graphs will vary but should reflect an understanding of the different characters.

Name: _____

Working With Words

An analogy is a comparison. Study this example:

Staunchly is to firmly as constricted is to __b__.   Relationship: Synonyms
a. loosened   b. contracted   c. surveyed   d. fidgeted

The first two underlined words, *staunchly* and *firmly*, are synonyms; therefore, the last two words must also be synonyms. *Contracted* is a synonym for *constricted*.

When completing an analogy, decide what the relationship between the first two words is. Find the same relationship for the next set of words.

Identify the relationship in each analogy. Then write the correct letter for each analogy below.

1. Tranquil is to peaceful as teeming is to _____.
   a. empty   b. hot   c. crowded   d. calm
   Relationship: _____

2. Melancholy is to sadness as ponderous is to _____.
   a. sorrow   b. smooth   c. pleasant   d. heavy
   Relationship: _____

3. Furrowed is to wrinkled as lounged is to _____.
   a. lunged   b. relaxed   c. hurried   d. furry
   Relationship: _____

4. Acrid is to mild as remorseless is to _____.
   a. merciful   b. acid   c. implored   d. bovine
   Relationship: _____

5. Jaunty is to droopy as perilous is to _____.
   a. perky   b. safe   c. prostrate   d. perfect
   Relationship: _____

6. Anguish is to joy as burly is to _____.
   a. husky   b. pain   c. pretty   d. weak
   Relationship: _____

7. Revulsion is to attraction as elation is to _____.
   a. despair   b. height   c. happiness   d. gallows
   Relationship: _____

8. Verandah is to porch as constable is to _____.
   a. prisoner   b. jail   c. sheriff   d. patio
   Relationship: _____

Name: _____

And Then…

Complete the chart below by adding causes or effects to show how events in the story are linked.

Cause	Effect
1.	The Tucks become ageless.
2. Winnie sees Jesse drink from the spring and wants a drink too.	
3.	The Fosters agree to sell their wood to the stranger.
4. The stranger threatens to take Winnie and sell the spring water.	
5. The constable says Mae will hang from the gallows.	
6. Winnie's adventure becomes known in Treegap.	
7.	Winnie doesn't marry Jesse and dies a natural death.

15

Name: _____

Where Do You Stand?

Consider two events from the story—helping Mae escape, and drinking the spring water—from the point of view of the characters named below. Then fill in each bar graph to show how you think they felt about each event.

1. Helping Mae escape.

From the point of view of:	Not at all justified				Entirely justified	
	0	1	2	3	4	5
Winnie						
the constable						
the Tucks						
the Foster family						
you						

2. Drinking the spring water.

From the point of view of:	Not at all justified				Entirely justified	
	0	1	2	3	4	5
Jesse						
Winnie						
Tuck						
man in yellow suit						
you						